SOJOURNER TRUTH

Slave, Abolitionist, Fighter for Women's Rights

SOJOURNER TRUTH

Slave, Abolitionist, Fighter for Women's Rights

by Aletha Jane Lindstrom

Illustrated by Paul Frame

JULIAN MESSNER NEW YORK

Published by Julian Messner, a Simon & Schuster
Division of Gulf & Western Corporation, Simon &
Schuster Building, 1230 Avenue of the Americas,
New York, N.Y. 10020.

JULIAN MESSNER and colophon are trademarks of Simon
& Schuster, registered in the U.S. Patent and Trade-
mark Office.

Manufactured in the United States of America

Designed by Alex D'Amato

Library of Congress Cataloging in Publication Data

Lindstrom, Aletha Jane.
　Sojourner Truth, slave, abolitionist, fighter for
women's rights.

　Includes index.
　SUMMARY: A biography of a former slave who became
one the best-known abolitionists of her day and spent
her life trying to improve living conditions for blacks.
　1. Truth, Sojourner, d. 1883—Juvenile literature.
2. Afro-Americans—Biography—Juvenile literature.
3. Abolitionists—United States—Biography—Juvenile
literature.　4. Social reformers—United States—
Biography—Juvenile literature.　[1. Truth, Sojourner,
d. 1883.　2. Afro-Americans—Biography.
3. Abolitionists.　4. Reformers]　I. Frame, Paul,
1913-　　　II. Title.
E185.97.T8L56　　　361.2'4'0924　[B]　[92]　79-25576
ISBN 0-671-32988-X

To

Berenice Bryant Lowe

Contents

SOJOURNER TRUTH
Slave, Abolitionist, Fighter for Women's Rights

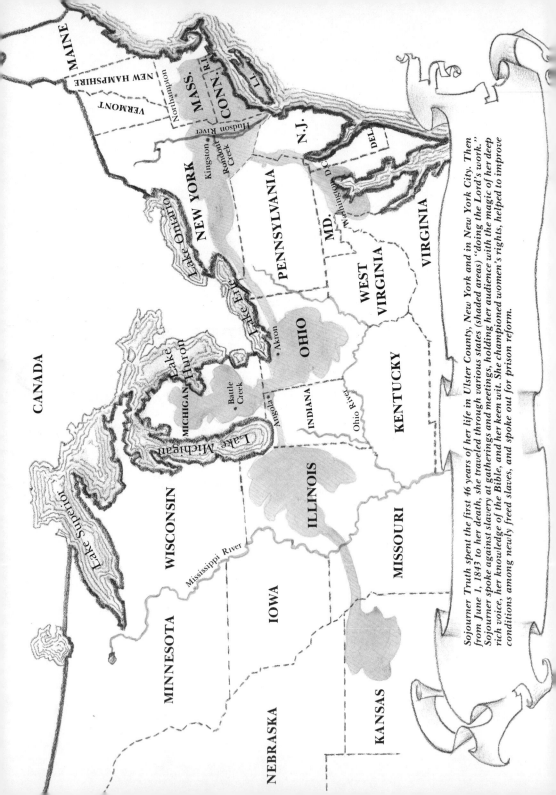

CANADA

MAINE

NEW HAMPSHIRE

VERMONT

Northampton

MASS.
CONN.
R.I.
L.I.

Hudson River

Kingston
Rondout Creek

NEW YORK

N.J.

Lake Ontario

Lake Erie

PENNSYLVANIA

DEL.

MD.
Washington D.C.

WEST VIRGINIA

VIRGINIA

Lake Superior

Lake Huron

Lake Michigan

MICHIGAN

Battle Creek

Akron

OHIO

Angola

INDIANA

Ohio River

KENTUCKY

Mississippi River

MINNESOTA

WISCONSIN

IOWA

ILLINOIS

MISSOURI

NEBRASKA

KANSAS

Sojourner Truth spent the first 46 years of her life in Ulster County, New York and in New York City. Then from June 1, 1843 to her death, she traveled through various states (shaded areas) "doing the Lord's work." Sojourner spoke against slavery at gatherings and meetings, holding her audience with the magic of her deep rich voice, her knowledge of the Bible, and her keen wit. She championed women's rights, helped to improve conditions among newly freed slaves, and spoke out for prison reform.

CHAPTER ONE

"What Will Become of Us Now?"

Belle woke with a start from a troubled sleep. She listened for a moment, her heart pounding. Then she reached over and gently shook her little brother.

"Peter," she whispered, "do you hear someone crying?"

"No, Belle," Peter said drowsily. "I don't hear anything."

Belle sat up on the straw-covered boards and looked around. The pine knot that supplied both heat and light for the slave cellar had nearly burned itself out. Its dying glow flickered over the ten other Hardenbergh slaves sleeping nearby. Everything seemed the same. Perhaps she'd been dreaming. Ma-Ma Bett, her and Peter's mother, wasn't with them. She was upstairs in the big house caring for the sick master. But Baumfree, their father, was sleeping in his usual place beside Peter.

11

Baumfree groaned and turned painfully in his sleep. His rheumatism was bad tonight. It was always worse when water oozed up between the loose floor boards and soaked the straw that the Hardenbergh slaves scattered about for bedding.

But Belle was accustomed to her father's groans. Something else had awakened her. There—she heard it again. Someone *was* crying. The sound came from above, just outside the cellar window.

The young slave girl pushed the tattered cover from her long, thin legs. Silently she crept up the steps, lifted the heavy trap door and slipped out into the moonlit yard.

Ma-Ma Bett sat huddled on a bench near the door. Tears streamed down her cheeks.

"Oh, Ma-Ma, is Master Charles going to die?" Belle asked, her voice trembling.

Ma-Ma Bett nodded. "Yes, Belle," she said between sobs. "Nothing more we can do for him now." She drew her little daughter down beside her and held her close.

Soon Ma-Ma Bett returned to the master's bedside, and Belle went back to the cellar. She moved across a gap in the boards close to Peter and pulled the blanket over them both.

But she couldn't sleep. Terror filled her heart. What would happen to them without Master Charles? Most slaves, Belle knew, were sold when a master died. And what about their father, Baumfree? Would he be

Ma-Ma Bett comforted Belle when she heard that Master Charles was going to die.

turned out to wander alone in the hills? Belle had heard of masters doing this to slaves who were too old to work.

The name "Baumfree" meant "strong and straight as a tree" in Dutch, the language spoken by the slaves and most of their masters here in the Dutch-settled Hudson River valley. In his youth, Baumfree had been one of the tallest, most powerful slaves in Ulster County. But Belle remembered her father only as a kindly old man whose body was twisted and bent from hard work and exposure to damp and cold. His spirit was broken from much sorrow. Two wives and many children had been sold from him before his slave "marriage" to Ma-Ma Bett. And he and Ma-Ma Bett had had twelve children sold away by former masters. Now only Belle and Peter were left.

Belle was born on the estate of Colonel Johannes Hardenbergh of Ulster County, New York State. She was born in the late 1700's. Belle never knew the day or year of her birth. Slave owners thought of their human property as livestock, like cattle or sheep. Therefore, they seldom bothered to record a slave's birthdate.

Ma-Ma Bett named her little girl Isabella, but everyone called her Belle. Colonel Hardenbergh must have been pleased with this new baby. She was strong and healthy. She would make an excellent field hand, or bring a good price if he decided to sell her.

Belle couldn't remember Colonel Hardenbergh. He died when she was very young. After the old master's death, his slaves became the property of his son, Charles

14

Hardenbergh. Charles moved them to his home in nearby Hurley.

"We were lucky to go to Master Charles," Belle heard her mother say many times. "He is by far the best of the Hardenberghs. He never beats or sells a slave. He doesn't believe in breaking up families."

Charles Hardenbergh's most trusted slaves were Ma-Ma Bett and Baumfree. He even allowed them to work a small piece of his land during the evenings. They could keep what they raised or exchange it for other goods.

The slaves felt safe with Master Charles, but with his illness this feeling of safety vanished. Daily they prayed for his recovery. Their prayers, however, were not to be answered.

Ma-Ma Bett came to the cellar at dawn with news of the master's death. All that day the bewildered slaves huddled together, crying and praying.

"What will become of us?" they asked each other over and over. And there in the dark cellar they told stories Belle had heard many times. But today, with the master dead, these stories took on new, frightening meaning to the girl crouched in the shadows beside her brother.

Ma-Ma Bett's sister-in-law, Betsey, told of a slave named Joe who took his three young sons and hid in the mountains. Old Master had sold Joe's wife. Joe was afraid he would sell his little boys, too. They were never heard of again. Some of the slaves believed they had starved to death. Others thought they were living with the Mohawk Indians.

Old Caesar, Betsey's husband, repeated a tale of a small slave boy who screamed and ran to his parents when the trader came to take him. The master grabbed the child and smashed his head against a stone wall. An Indian passed by while the mother was preparing her son for burial. "If I'd been there," he said, "I'd have sunk my tomahawk in the murderer's skull."

But the slaves in the cellar agreed that the child should have gone quietly, and the parents should have shown no grief. "Masters get angry when slaves look sad or make a fuss," Betsey said. "Better to save the tears until white folks aren't around."

Ma-Ma Bett and Baumfree spoke in sad voices of their many "lost children." They wept silently when they mentioned the last two, Michel and Nancy. They were even younger than Belle and Peter when a trader drove up in a red sleigh one winter morning. Old Master put the children in the sleigh box and slammed the cover down. As the sleigh pulled out of the yard, the youngsters' terrified screams mingled with the merry sound of jingling bells. Ma-Ma Bett and Baumfree never knew what happened to these two, or to any of their other children.

Now, as Belle listened, terror clutched her like an icy hand. She put her arms around Peter and held him close. Would slave traders come for her and Peter now that Master Charles was dead? Would they, too, be taken from their father and mother and sold?

That night, the parents took the two children up into the yard. "Look at the stars and the moon," Ma-Ma Bett said. "Those are the same stars and that is the same moon that look down on your brothers and sisters. No matter how far we are from them or from each other, we can always see the same stars and the same moon."

Under the night sky, Belle and Peter learn about God from their parents.

"And remember, children," Ma-Ma Bett continued, "there is a God who sees and hears you."

"God, Ma-Ma?" Belle asked. "Where does He live?"

"He lives in the sky. He is everywhere. When you are beaten or cruelly treated, you must ask Him for help. He will always hear and help you."

"'You must not steal." Ma-Ma Bett went on. "You must not lie. And you must always obey your master. Now, Belle and Peter, kneel in front of me and fold your hands." The children knelt. Together they repeated the Lord's Prayer: "Our Father which art in heaven. . . ."

Then Baumfree lifted Peter, his last little son. Belle followed them down to the dark, evil-smelling cellar. The two children snuggled close together in the damp straw. Baumfree gently tucked the soiled, ragged blanket around them.

Before Belle fell asleep, she whispered the Lord's Prayer to herself. This prayer—and the words her mother spoke that night—were to help her endure the cruelties that lay ahead. They were to become the guiding force of her life.

CHAPTER TWO

The Auction

A few days after Charles Hardenbergh's death, notices appeared in Kingston, the county seat, that the slaves, sheep, horses and cattle of Charles Hardenbergh would be auctioned off the following week.

Notices of slave auctions, once common in New York State, now appeared only occasionally. Slavery was dying out in New York. It had already been outlawed in all other northern states, except New Jersey, since shortly after the Revolutionary War.

Slavery continued to flourish in the South where farming went on throughout the year. But in the North, with its short growing seasons, slavery was proving impractical. There was little farm work for slaves in the long winters. And whether they had work to do or not, they had to be housed and fed.

Then, too, manufacturing was becoming increasingly important in the North. Farmers and factory owners alike were finding it cheaper to hire free laborers. They didn't have to be furnished food and housing, and they could be laid off during slack seasons.

Also, the Quakers, a religious group, strongly opposed slavery. In their quiet way, they were making life increasingly difficult for slave owners.

But the fact that slavery was doomed in New York meant little to the frightened Hardenbergh slaves. To them, as to most slaves, an auction was a terrible affair.

Charles Hardenbergh's brothers were inheriting his property. They had their worries, too. A slave auction should bring a profit. But that elderly couple, Caesar and Betsey, probably wouldn't sell. And who would want crippled, half-blind old Baumfree?

"We could give him his freedom," one of the Hardenberghs said. The others shook their heads. Then they would have to post a bond so he wouldn't become a burden on the county. No one wanted to put up the money.

While they were deciding about Baumfree, John Hardenbergh agreed to take Caesar and Betsey. They could do chores around his property.

"Let's free Ma-Ma Bett and make her legally responsible for Baumfree," someone suggested. "She looks able to support him, and that arrangement will satisfy the law." Since Ma-Ma Bett would probably sell for less than the amount of the bond, the family agreed.

Ma-Ma Bett and Baumfree could scarcely believe their good fortune. Freedom! All their lives they had prayed for it. For a moment they forgot that Belle and

Peter wouldn't share their freedom.

Peter sold quickly. He was strong, and young enough to be easily trained. His new owner whisked him away through the crowd before his parents and Belle realized he had been sold.

Belle, probably nine years old at the time, was next. The shy young girl had known only kindness from her parents and the other Hardenbergh slaves. What happened now was like a nightmare. She would remember it with horror all her life.

Strangers pushed her toward the auction block, and the auctioneer started his chant. Prospective buyers ran rough hands over her body and pinched her muscles. They forced their fingers into her mouth to inspect her teeth and gums. Then they tore her dress from her back to inspect it for scars—the sure sign of a troublesome slave.

The auctioneer was quick to point out that here was a tall, healthy female of good stock. In a few years, she could manage a household or do a man's work in the fields.

Strangely, no one bid on her. It might have been the rebellious set of the chin or the dreamy, sensitive dark eyes. Perhaps it was the look of exceptional intelligence on the small frightened face that turned possible buyers away; a stupid slave was so much easier to manage.

At last the disgusted auctioneer pushed her aside and called for the livestock. What happened next was a

confused blur to Belle. She was vaguely aware that someone bid a hundred dollars for a flock of sheep. "Sold!" the
auctioneer shouted, and banged his hammer down. Then
he shoved Belle toward the thin-faced buyer, a man by the
name of John Neely. "Here," he said, "take the black
wench along with the sheep!"

Belle heard her father's voice and looked around.
Baumfree was pushing his way through the crowd.
"Belle," he cried, "be a good girl, and do what Mr. Neely

Belle is sold at auction.

says. It's not far to your new place. We're free now. We'll come to see you soon."

Before Baumfree could reach Belle, her new owner shouted a harsh command and prodded her in the back. Blinded by tears and dust, the little black girl followed the frightened, bleating sheep through the gate and out into the road.

"Not far to your new place," her father had said. But to Belle, stumbling up and down hills and across

tumbling streams, the way seemed endless. She longed to run back to her parents. But this cruel-faced stranger now owned her completely, just as he owned the confused sheep milling about her.

During the excitement of the auction, Neely had been pleased with his purchase. Now, as he neared home, he began to have serious doubts. That snuffling, stumbling black gal was plenty tall, but she was about as scrawny as a picked chicken. Maybe that fast-talking Dutch auctioneer had outsmarted him after all. And Mrs. Neely had her heart set on a white servant. She might not take kindly to a black young'un who, like as not, spoke only Dutch.

The English-speaking Neelys hated the Dutch. The childless couple, newcomers to the area, had recently set up a boat landing and store on Rondout Creek, near Kingston. Their business would have been doing well, but for one thing. The Neelys found themselves in the midst of Dutch farmers. The clannish Dutch didn't like to have Yankees settle in their valley. They stayed away from the Neelys and their store.

Mrs. Neely was waiting in the yard. Her sour glance went from the dusty, bedraggled child to her husband. "What you got there, John Neely?"

"A black gal to help you with the chores. Thought maybe owning a slave would make those stupid Dutch farmers feel a little more kindly toward us."

Sharp, angry words poured out of Mrs. Neely. Belle couldn't understand their meaning, but she was well aware that Mrs. Neely was furious with her husband for bringing a black child home. Belle shrank before the scorn in her new mistress's voice and the hatred in her eyes.

Many years later, Belle, recalling that moment, said, "Now the war began."

CHAPTER THREE

New Masters

From the first, Belle's days were filled with slappings, scoldings and sharp, confusing commands. Mrs. Neely would shout and wave toward the cooking utensils. Belle, not understanding, would scurry and bring the pot hooks. Then she would receive a clout on the head because her mistress had wanted the frying pan.

Belle had plenty to eat, but she suffered terribly from the harsh winter. Her only garment was of slave cloth with holes for her head and arms. This offered little warmth inside the drafty house. Outside it was no protection at all against the cruel wind and deep snow. She had firewood to fetch, and the pigs, sheep and chickens to tend. She had no shoes so that her frostbitten feet were covered with deep, raw cracks.

Then there were the beatings. The worst of these occurred one Sunday morning. For no apparent reason Mr. Neely dragged her to the barn, tied her hands and bared her back. Then he reached for a bundle of slender wooden rods. He had burned them in embers until they were as smooth and hard as iron. Towering above the child, he let loose the anger that had been building in him for months. When the first blow fell, Belle screamed. The next came harder. Trying to stifle her sobs, she clenched her hands until the nails cut the flesh. Then, mercifully, she fainted.

When she came to, she was lying in a pool of her own blood. She lay there, sobbing, for a long time. She cried because she hurt so and because she was homesick. At last she remembered Ma-Ma Bett's promise—God would help her if she asked Him.

Toward dusk she staggered to a field far from the house. Kneeling in the snow, she turned her small face upward. Then she shouted with all her strength, "God, do You think it was right to let Master whip me like that? If I was You and You was me, I wouldn't let it happen to You. I know I been bad sometimes, but not that bad. Please, God, make my master and missus good or get me new ones. Seems like I can't stand much more." Then, because she was so homesick, she added, "And please let my daddy come like he promised. It's been such a long time."

Days passed. Nothing changed. Perhaps God hadn't heard her through the thick clouds. Or maybe even God couldn't make the Neelys good.

Then one late winter afternoon, Belle heard a farm wagon rattle down the frozen road. The white driver paused at the gate and helped an old man out. Belle

Hurt and homesick, Belle prayed to God for help.

looked, and looked again. "Daddy!" she cried and ran to meet him. "God," she whispered, "you did hear me after all!"

Baumfree leaned heavily on Belle as he stumbled toward the kitchen door. Inside, on an old bench, Belle snuggled close. "I wanted to come before," her father said, "but I've been too poorly to walk. Mr. Simmons brought me today. He had an errand down the road. The Simmonses are renting the big house and letting us stay in the cellar."

And Ma-Ma Bett?

She, too, was poorly. The winter, and losing her children, had been hard on her. She was too sick to come.

Peter, had he seen Peter? Belle wanted to know.

Baumfree shook his head. "They took him over twenty miles away, Belle. Too far for an old man to walk. Don't expect I'll see my boy again."

When it was time for Mr. Simmons to return, Belle helped her father to the gate. There, out of Mrs. Neely's sight, she showed him the deep cuts on her back.

Baumfree was horrified. "You being a good girl, Belle?" he asked as he gently touched the welts with his stiff, crippled fingers.

"Oh, Daddy," Belle sobbed, "I try, but I don't even know what the Neelys say. Daddy, can't you get me a new place?"

Baumfree held her close. "I'll try, Belle," he said. Then it was time to go.

When the wagon was out of sight, Belle looked down. There in the snow were the marks from Baumfree's boots. Each day, until the snow melted, she returned and placed her bare feet in the footprints. Standing there, she could remember her father's arms around her. Somehow this helped her through the days that seemed to drag on endlessly.

❖❖❖❖❖❖❖❖❖❖❖❖❖❖❖❖❖❖❖❖❖❖❖❖❖❖

Baumfree wasted no time. Each kindly soul he met, black or white, heard of the Neelys' cruelty. One spring day, Belle was gathering firewood in the yard. She looked up and saw a tall stranger approaching. A smile brightened his gentle, weather-beaten face. "Well, little girl," he asked in the Dutch language that was music to her ears, "would you like to come and live with me?"

Belle's heart had been heavy for such a long time. Suddenly it was as light as the lambs' wool clouds in the blue sky. "Oh, yes!" she breathed. "Oh, yes!"

She didn't even need to return to the hated house. Her only possession was the garment she was wearing.

Martin Schryver mounted his horse. "Come along, then," he said cheerily. Belle trotted behind him like a devoted puppy. Once again God had answered a prayer.

Like her former owners, Belle's new master lived in Ulster County. With his wife and two sons, he operated a tavern near Kingston. They also did a little farming and fishing.

Martin Schryver owned no slaves. He bought Belle simply because she was being abused. She cost him one hundred and five dollars.

30

The years with the Schryvers were the happiest of Belle's life. She spent hours beside Rondout Creek watching Indian canoes glide silently past, and sailing vessels come and go. Frequently she was awakened at dawn to help unload the fishing boats. She planted and hoed corn, and searched the woods for the herbs Mrs. Schryver used in her beers. When supplies ran short, it was Belle who trotted to the store near the boat landing for a jug of molasses or liquor. Because she was happy, she sang— African songs that Ma-Ma Bett had learned from her mother.

Belle had been with the Schryvers for around two years when Ma-Ma Bett died. Mr. Simmons came for her. The past winter had been hard on her parents, he told her. Their food and firewood had lasted only until Christmas. After that, they had gotten along with the little he and his wife could spare. Even the warm summer hadn't restored Ma-Ma Bett's strength. The day of her death Baumfree had been raking behind hay wagons to earn a few pennies. He came home expecting bread and baked apples for supper. At the bottom of the cellar steps, he stumbled over Ma-Ma Bett's body.

Belle grieved for her mother, and her heart ached for her crippled, half-blind father. The freedom the two had welcomed with such joy had come too late. Freedom at their age, when they could no longer care for themselves, had been a cruel gift. "Oh," Baumfree said again and again. "I thought God would take me first. I am so old and helpless."

Belle returned to the tavern with a deeply troubled heart. A short time later, when she was serving customers, John Dumont, a prosperous gentleman farmer from New Paltz, also in Ulster County, stopped by for a mug of ale. He spoke pleasantly to Belle in English quite different from the rough language, laced with cursing, that she had picked up from the fishermen and lumberjacks who came to the tavern. When Dumont finished his drink, he beckoned to Belle's owner. "Three hundred dollars for that gal," he said.

Martin Schryver blinked. Three hundred dollars for a spindly child? But she was no longer a child, he noted with surprise. She was nearly six feet tall and moved with self-confident grace. Not exactly beautiful—her face was too broad for beauty—but there was something compelling about the luminous eyes and soft, rich voice.

The tavern keeper sighed. He was fond of Belle, and he had come to depend on her more than he realized. But money was tight, and he needed a new fishing boat. Then, too, Dumont was known to be considerate of his slaves. Reluctantly, Schryver signed the bill of sale.

CHAPTER FOUR

"Lord, What Is This Slavery?"

John Dumont bought Belle in 1810. He noted the date in his journal and added that she appeared to be about 13 years old and unusually tall for her age.

Recalling Mr. Neely's floggings, Belle was determined to please her new owners. All might have gone well if she had worked only in the fields with Dumont's ten other slaves. But she had housework to do, also.

Mrs. Dumont disliked Belle. The woman had come from a family that did not own slaves, and she mistrusted all blacks. She much preferred her white bond servant, Kate. The two of them did their best, as Belle later expressed it, "to grind her down."

However, Dumont was delighted with his new purchase. "Why that black wench, will do the family washing before dawn and then put in a full day in the field," he boasted.

"She may work long hours," Mrs. Dumont admitted with a shrug, "but her work is usually only half-done."

One morning at breakfast, Mrs. Dumont thrust a dish of potatoes under her husband's nose. "They're dirty," she said. "It's the way Belle does all her work."

"I can't understand it, Master," Belle said. "I scrubbed them clean, put them on to cook, and went to the barn to do the milking, just as always."

The next morning they were dirty again. Dumont scolded Belle, and canceled a promised visit to her father. But Gertrude, Dumont's little daughter, liked Belle and disliked Kate. The third morning when Belle came in from the barn, she heard Gertrude announce gleefully, "It's Kate, Daddy. I saw her throw dirt in the potatoes. She just wants to get Belle in trouble."

Mrs. Dumont sniffed and said nothing, but her husband looked pleased. "You may visit your father on Sunday," he told Belle. "And you can use the wagon."

On the way to the Simmonses', Belle came upon an old Negro with hair as white as snow, resting by the roadside. Belle climbed down from the wagon and went to him. It was Baumfree. She could scarcely believe how much he had failed since Ma-Ma Bett's death. His eyesight was so poor that he didn't know Belle until she spoke. Then he clung to her while tears streamed down his wrinkled cheeks.

He was on his way to John Hardenbergh's, he told her. With Ma-Ma Bett dead, he was once more the Hardenbergh family's legal responsibility. They "took turns" keeping him. When he moved from one family to the next, he went on foot with his staff to guide him. Sometimes the distance was over ten miles. Frequently, a passing farmer gave him a lift.

With the sun warm on their backs, they sat on a large stone and visited. Baumfree spoke of how much he missed her and Peter. But he talked mostly of Ma-Ma Bett and his loneliness without her.

According to a New York law passed in 1817, all New York slaves born before July 4, 1799 would be set free on Freedom Day, July 4, 1827. Children born after 1799 were considered born free, but they must remain as unpaid servants of the mother's owner until age twenty-five for girls and age twenty-eight for boys. Since Belle was born before 1799, she would be freed in 1827.

Belle thought of this coming freedom as she spoke to her father. "Just wait, Daddy," she said. "White folks at Dumont's are saying that all us slaves will be free in maybe fifteen years or so. Then I can care for you just as Ma-Ma Bett did."

Baumfree looked at Belle and shook his head. "Fifteen years you say, Daughter? I can't wait that long."

"But Daddy, you can if you try. You've got to live until then."

Baumfree shook his head again and fumbled for his staff. Belle helped him into the wagon and drove him to Hardenberghs'.

On her way to visit her father, Belle met him by the roadside.

Now Belle worked harder than ever, hoping to be rewarded by visits to her father. Her desire to please was so great that she often worked all day and most of the night, stopping only to nap in a chair.

"White folks' nigger," her fellow slaves taunted. "Making the rest of us look lazy." But Belle ignored them. She wanted to please only this master who completely controlled her life. Somehow he seemed to know everything his slaves did. He rewarded them when they were good, and punished them when they were bad. Dumont fitted Ma-Ma Bett's description of God. In fact, Belle half-believed he was God.

But in spite of her hard work, Belle rarely visited Baumfree. "Can't spare you right now, Belle," Dumont would say. "Maybe next week. . . ."

Lonely, and worried about her father, Belle began going daily to a clump of willows near the creek. Here she sang songs to lift her spirits, and she talked to God about her troubles. She gained comfort from this even though she wasn't sure where God was, or who He was.

One evening, a slave from the adjoining farm was mending fence on the opposite bank. Belle was now about sixteen, the stranger probably a few years older. "Hello," he said, wading across and holding out his hand. "I'm Catlin's Bob."

"And I'm Dumont's Belle." As if by magic, her loneliness vanished.

The two met frequently in this secluded spot. Soon

they were in love. "Maybe our masters will let us get married," Bob said. "Then on Freedom Day we can get married again, a real marriage that some old master can't break up."

And so, briefly, they were happy. But when Catlin learned that his young slave was courting Belle, he flew into a rage. "Pick a girl from my place," he ordered Bob. "Then your babies will be mine, not Dumont's. Go there again and I'll half kill you."

Bob did go again one day, to inquire about Belle when he heard she was ill. Catlin and his sons followed. Belle heard a commotion outside the slave quarters. From the window she watched with horror as the three men beat Bob about the head with heavy canes until blood poured down his body.

Dumont rushed out. "Lay off!" he cried. "I'll have no slave killed on my property!"

They tied Bob with ropes and dragged him home. Belle never saw him again. Later she learned that he died a short time after the flogging.

"It's time you started a family, Belle," Dumont said one day. So he married her to Thomas, an old slave on the place. Belle offered no resistance. A slave was expected to bear babies to increase her master's stock. And with Bob dead, it made no difference whom she married.

After Belle's first child, Diana, was born, Dumont gave the young mother permission to visit Baumfree. Belle walked twelve miles carrying her baby, only to learn that her father was no longer with the Hardenbergh families. Tired of the old slave, they had freed Caesar and Betsy and sent all three to live in a cabin in the Catskill Mountains. Wearily, Belle retraced her steps to Dumonts'.

Before she had a chance to see her father, word arrived of his death. At the funeral, Belle learned that Caesar and Betsey had died soon after moving to the cabin. Baumfree, totally blind and scarcely able to move, was left to shift for himself. A stranger passed the cabin one morning and stopped to investigate. He found Baumfree's frozen body lying on a filthy cot.

"It was cruel of the Hardenberghs to abandon the old man," someone said in a guarded voice.

"Others have done worse," came the soft reply. "Lots of old, worn-out slaves are left in the hills to die, without even a cabin for shelter."

John Hardenbergh joined Belle as she followed the coffin down the mountain. "Nothing too good for old Baumfree," he said."He was a hardworking, faithful servant. We're giving him a fine burial."

So Baumfree was buried in a pine box painted black instead of the usual slave coffin of unpainted boards. John Hardenbergh, himself, led the few ragged mourners in the Lord's Prayer: "Forgive us our debts, as we forgive our debtors. . . ." Then he passed a jug of his best corn whiskey to raise the spirits of the forlorn little group gathered around the grave.

Belle pushed the jug away. Suddenly she felt sick. She thought of her parents, their miserable lives, and then abandoned to die after there was no work left in their worn-out bodies. Ma-Ma Bett had always believed that Blacks were intended by God to be slaves of white men. Belle had believed this, too. Now, as she turned away from her father's grave, she whispered, "Oh, God, what is this slavery that does such terrible things? What evil can it not do?"

CHAPTER FIVE

A Master's Promise

Within the next few years two more children, Peter and Elizabeth, were born to Belle. Small Peter was Belle's favorite, probably because he reminded her of the little brother sold at the long-ago auction.

Mrs. Dumont resented each new baby, but her husband was very fond of Belle's children. When Dumont came in the house and heard a child crying, he turned on

his wife angrily. "Why do you keep Belle at her work when her baby needs her? Belle, take care of your children, if you do nothing else all week."

Belle preferred working in the fields, away from Mrs. Dumont. Here she solved the problem of infant care in a way common to slave mothers. She hung the baby's basket from a low branch of a tree near where she was working. Then a child, who was too young for labor, gently swung the basket, lulling the baby to sleep.

When Belle looked at her children, she often thought of Ma-Ma Bett and her "lost children." But Belle felt sure that Dumont would never sell one of hers. She was deeply grateful to this god-like master.

While she worked in the fields, Belle could also take care of her baby.

Thomas, her husband, felt no gratitude. He and the other slaves were looking forward to Freedom Day. "Can't no master go back on this promise," Thomas said. "This is the law, and the law is bigger than any master."

Belle shook her head. She understood about Freedom Day. But the law? What was that? How could anything be bigger than a master? Bigger than Dumont?

One morning Dumont said to Belle, "You've been my best worker. If you continue to work hard, I'll free you and Thomas a year ahead of the others."

Thomas scoffed when she told him. "That's just an old master trick to get more work out of you. Dumont ain't going to free a good worker like you till he has to."

Belle said nothing. Now that her parents were dead, she felt no need for freedom. Her children must remain with Dumont; she preferred to remain, too.

Then one day, Belle returned from the fields and found that five-year-old Peter was gone. Dumont, possibly drunk at the time, had sold the child to a Dr. Gedney. Gedney was leaving for England with friends. He thought the little boy would be a helpful and entertaining addition to the group.

Belle was shocked when Thomas told her. She hurried straight to the house and entered Mr. Dumont's study. For the first time in her life she spoke to a white person without waiting for permission. "Master," she said, "you had no right to sell my son. He's too little to be away from me."

"The law gives me the right to sell your son, Belle,"

44

Dumont replied. "Not sell him exactly, but sell his services until he is twenty-eight."

Dumont fidgeted with some papers. He already regretted selling Peter. He'd miss the little boy. Besides, if by some chance Gedney sold Peter out of state, there could be serious trouble with the law. Now he shrugged his shoulders. "I can't get him back, Belle. What's done is done."

Belle's eyes never left his face. "Master, when do I get my freedom?"

Dumont looked surprised. "Next July fourth, about a year from now. That is, if you work hard until then."

"Never fear, Master. I'll work hard."

Dumont watched as she left the room. *She's always walked tall and proud*, he thought. But today there was something else—an air of determination. He sighed and reached for his journal. All these slaves were getting uppity, now that Freedom Day was approaching. But he hadn't expected it of Belle.

How long was a year? How long until freedom? Slaves had no calendars to keep track of days. They measured time by seasons, by work to be done. Now Belle figured she'd be free about the time next summer's hay was stored in the great high barn. Dr. Gedney should be back with Peter soon after that. If she were free, she could find Peter and keep in touch with him, even if she couldn't have him back.

It was difficult for Belle to work that year. She had a new baby, Sophie, to care for. And she slashed her

45

forefinger with a scythe. Because she continued to use her hand, the deep, jagged cut became infected and didn't heal properly. Sometimes she could scarcely endure the throbbing pain. But she did her share, and more, of Dumont's work.

On July fourth she asked Dumont for her freedom.

"I'm sorry, Belle," he said. "I can't get along without you. Besides, with that bad hand and a new baby, you haven't kept your part of the bargain."

Belle thought of the long hours she had worked in spite of her crippled hand and the baby's needs. "Master," she said, "you know I've done my work, same as I promised."

Dumont turned away. "You'll stay. There's much work to do."

So Thomas had been right after all. Dumont had tricked her. How could she ever have believed that he was God? He wasn't as good as she, his slave. She'd never lied to Dumont, but he had lied to her. And she'd never stolen, not even a crust of bread for a hungry child. But her master had stolen years from her life, and he'd stolen her little son and sold him away.

Belle had made a promise to Dumont, and she had kept that promise. Now she made a promise to herself. This one, too, she intended to keep. She would take her freedom. And Ma-Ma Bett's God would help her. He would know that she was right.

CHAPTER SIX

A Hullabaloo Over a Little Nigger

Belle didn't leave in July. First she helped harvest the crops. Then she washed and spun the year's supply of wool, and wrapped it on spools. It was fall before she felt she could leave with a clear conscience.

Still she lingered. "It's like this, Lord," she prayed. "I'm afraid to go at night, and if I leave by day, they'll be after me for sure."

Suddenly she knew what to do. She could leave just before daylight and be miles away before folks were awake. "Thank you, God," Belle said. "That's a good idea."

It was hard to leave her two little girls. But Diana was now eight and used to taking care of one-year-old Elizabeth and keeping her out of Mrs. Dumont's way. And Dumont was always kind to the children. Belle felt sure he would let no harm come to them.

Early one October morning, she took Sophie in her arms and slipped quietly out of the slave quarters. The moon cast a dim light so she kept to the shadows at the road's edge. After several hours, the road led upward, through thick woods. She reached the top of a hill and stepped out into full sunlight. Never had she known a dawn so bright. Far below lay the valley, veiled in shining mist. Belle felt overjoyed with a new sense of freedom. Then came a sobering thought. "Oh, God," she prayed, "where can I go?"

The mist thinned and sunlight fell on a white house in the valley. Belle headed toward it. Levi Rowe, a Quaker, lived there. He directed Belle to a Quaker couple, Isaac Van Wagener and his wife, who lived in nearby Wagondale. "They will be glad to take you in," Mr. Rowe told her.

Belle was thankful that the Van Wageners lived fairly close to Dumont. She knew that he would track her down. He had usually been kind to her, and she didn't want to put him to the trouble of a long, difficult search. Besides, at Van Wageners she would be near Diana and Elizabeth.

"Thee and thy child are most welcome here," Isaac Van Wagener told Belle. "We have employment for thee as long as thee has need of it." Mrs. Van Wagener directed Belle to a room with a clean white bed. "Oh, my!" Belle said to Sophie. "They can't mean for us to sleep in that

With baby Sophie in her arms, Belle left the Dumonts.

beautiful bed. Never slept in a bed in my life." She spent the night on the floor with Sophie in her arms.

The next morning Dumont arrived. "So you've run away from me, Belle," he said.

"No," Belle replied. "I walked away and only because you promised me a year of my time."

Dumont reached for Sophie. Belle drew back. She didn't know what to do. The baby was too little to be separated from her. But by law Dumont could claim the child.

A soft voice broke the silence. "Friend," Isaac Van Wagener said, "I do not hold with buying slaves, but rather than see Belle return to bondage, I will pay thee twenty dollars for Belle's services for the year and five more for the baby."

Dumont took the money and left. Belle turned to thank the Quaker. "Master . . ." she began.

"Please do not call me Master. There is only one Master in this house and thee and I both serve Him."

Belle helped with the housework and cared for Sophie. But soon she became bored with the peace and quiet. The kindly Quakers even shook their heads when Belle laughed loudly or sang. Such pleasures were considered worldly by these deeply religious people. Then, too, Belle grew increasingly lonesome for Diana and Elizabeth. And when spring arrived, she longed to be back at Dumonts' working in the sun-warmed fields.

One morning Belle announced to the surprised

Quakers, "Master is coming today, and I'm going home with him."

Strangely, Dumont arrived that afternoon. Belle was waiting with Sophie in her arms. "We're going home with you," she said.

As she approached the wagon, she seemed aware of a great, overpowering light. She stopped, unable to take another step. "Oh, Lord," she whispered, "it must be You. I didn't know You was so big."

She returned to her room and placed Sophie on the bed. Then, shaking with fear, she dropped to her knees. Surely God would strike her down for attempting to return to slavery. She thought, too, of her other sins, especially of her hatred for the Neelys and the Hardenberghs.

Nothing happened. Could it be that God had forgiven her? "Oh, God," she said, "if You can forgive me then I can forgive, too—even the white folks."

At last, free of her burden of hate, she went out into the yard. "The whole world grew bright," she said years later, "and the trees waved in glory. Every little stone on the ground shone like glass . . . and I began to feel such love in my soul . . . love for all creatures."

After this experience, Belle listened eagerly whenever Isaac Van Wagener read from the Bible. She had never heard of this book that told of God and his son, Jesus. She especially liked the words, "I am the Way, the Truth, and the Life."

On Freedom Day, Isaac Van Wagener gave Belle

her freedom papers and said, "God is no respecter of persons or color. Before God all of us are equal." Equal before God? Then surely, Belle reasoned, she must be the equal of any person, black or white.

Belle remained with the Van Wageners after Freedom Day, receiving a small wage for her services. Occasionally she worked for other families. If this work prevented her from taking Sophie with her she left the baby with Diana and Elizabeth at Dumonts'. The girls were always delighted to have their little sister. Mr. Dumont didn't object. And Mrs. Dumont didn't care how many Blacks were in the slave quarters, as long as they kept out of her kitchen.

Belle attended church services in the Quaker meeting house. She thought the quiet devotions of these people a strange way to worship the God of all creation.

One Sunday she passed a church where only whites were welcome. She was delighted to hear singing. This seemed the proper way to praise God. She returned several Sundays to stand outside and listen. Frequently she joined her own rich, sweet voice with those of the worshipers. One hymn remained a lifelong favorite. It reminded her of the glorious morning when she had taken her freedom:

> *It was early in the morning*
> *Just at the break of day,*
> *When He rose, when He rose, when He rose*
> *And went to heaven on a cloud.*

Weeks passed with no news of Peter. Then one Sunday, after services, Belle overheard someone mention that Dr. Gedney was home. She hurried to the Van Wageners'. Would they please take care of Sophie for a few days? She had to find Peter at once. Her employers agreed to care for Sophie.

Then Isaac Van Wagener's kindly face grew stern. "Belle," he said, "I hadn't intended to tell thee this at this time, but the Quakers hereabouts are greatly upset. Dr. Gedney didn't take Peter to England. He found him too small for his services and sent him back to Solomon Gedney, his brother. We fear Solomon defied the law and sold Peter out of state."

Belle didn't wait to hear more. *Dumont will know about this*, she thought. She ran all the way to New Paltz. Her former master wasn't home, but Mrs. Dumont listened impatiently. "Ugh," she said, "all this hullabaloo about a paltry little nigger. It's a pity they're not all in Africa! Why you've got more now than you can care for."

Belle's eyes blazed. "I'll have my child again!" she told Mrs. Dumont. In later years she said, "I felt so tall within. I felt that the power of the nation was in me!"

Next she hurried to Dr. Gedney's home. What she learned there made her heartsick. Solomon had sold Peter to his brother-in-law, Mr. Fowler. Fowler had taken the boy to his plantation in Alabama, a slave state in the deep South.

Utterly discouraged, Belle dragged homeward. Now Peter would never be free. Isaac Van Wagener said that Gedney had broken the law. But what was the law? And how could it help her—a black woman? Who would listen to her?

God would listen, she reminded herself. She knelt by the roadside and prayed for a long time. When twilight fell, she heard footsteps. She looked up and saw Dumont coming toward her. "I'm sorry about Peter," he said. "I can do nothing. But Quakers—friends of the Van Wageners'—live there." He pointed to a lighted house down the road. "Those people will help you. But don't mention my name or I'll be in trouble." He hurried off into the night.

The Quakers seemed to be expecting Belle. Next morning they took her to the courthouse in Kingston. Here Belle poured out her story to the grand jury. One of the group, Lawyer Chip, produced a Bible. "Will you swear on this that the child of whom you speak is your son?"

"Oh, yes!" Belle said eagerly.

Several jurors laughed. "She's a Negro. Her word is worth nothing."

"It will satisfy the law," Lawyer Chip said briefly. He prepared a writ for Belle to deliver to the constable in New Paltz. Belle ran the entire nine miles, clutching the precious paper. But the constable mistakenly served it on the wrong brother. Solomon Gedney, knowing he faced fourteen years in prison for selling Peter out of state, had already left for Alabama. He hoped to bring Peter back.

Gedney sailed from New York City in the fall. He returned with Peter the following spring. Though he had now given up all rights to the child, he refused to let Belle even see her son. Instead, he posted a $600 bond as security that he would appear in the next court session, which would be held in several months.

Again Belle went to Lawyer Chip. The lawyer smiled. "Why worry? If Gedney puts Peter out of the way, he must give up the six hundred dollars. Half of it will be yours." He looked at Belle's bare feet and coarse, ill-fitting dress. "Three hundred dollars will buy a heap of clothes."

"I don't want clothes," Belle said. "I want my son. He's been away from me too long already."

Lawyer Chip turned away. He was tired of this strange, stubborn black woman.

Once more the Quakers helped Belle. They gave her money for a new lawyer who brought the case to court in a few days. The judge decided that Peter should go with his mother.

Peter was in the courtroom. He fell to his knees in front of Solomon Gedney. "She's not my mother," he cried. "Please don't make me go with her!"

"What strange talk is this, Peter?" Belle asked. "Who has beaten these lies into you?"

"Peter," the judge said, "stop that screaming and go with your mother."

Outside Peter said, "Oh, Ma, Mr. Gedney said he'd beat me something fearful if I didn't say what he told me."

Belle touched the scars on Peter's face. "Let's go home," she said.

The judge gives Peter back to his mother.

CHAPTER SEVEN

Life in the City

Belle had accomplished an unheard of feat for a black woman in that year of 1828. She had taken a powerful white man to court and won her case. But Belle wasn't thinking of that when she left the courthouse with Peter. Her thoughts were all for her son. When they arrived at the Van Wageners', she removed his clothing. His entire body was covered with cuts and welts.

"Heavens," she whispered. "What's all this?"

"It's where Fowler whipped me, Ma," Peter said. "Sometimes I'd climb under the stoop to get away, and the blood would stick to the boards."

"Oh, Peter," Belle cried, "how could you bear it? What did Mrs. Fowler say?"

"She said she wished I was with you, Ma. When Fowler was asleep, she'd come and grease my sores. He was terrible when he was drunk. He beat her, too."

In spite of his mistreatment, Peter still had the appealing smile that Belle remembered so well. But there was a restlessness about the child that disturbed her. "He's going to be quite a handful," she admitted to Isaac Van

Wagener. "He needs something to keep him out of mischief."

With Mr. Van Wagener's help, she placed Peter with the man who worked the locks on Rondout Creek. This seemed an ideal spot for the boy. He loved to be around boats and barges. He was always talking about the graceful clipper ship with great white sails that brought him back from Alabama.

That summer, Miss Gear, a schoolteacher from New York City, vacationed in Ulster County. She was attracted by Peter's intelligence and happy disposition. Soon she was urging Belle to return to the city with her. There Peter could attend school. She would pay his expenses, she said, and find work for Belle. Peter begged his mother to accept the offer.

By summer's end, Belle had decided to go. There was no future for a black youth in Ulster County. School should keep Peter out of trouble, and it might lead to a promising career. Then, too, in the city she could earn double the wages she now received. Perhaps she could save enough to make a home for her children by the time the girls were old enough to leave John Dumont. She could not take Sophie with her, but the little girl already spent much of her time with Diana and Elizabeth. She could leave the baby with them. This arrangement was satisfactory with Dumont, too.

In the fall of 1829, Belle and Peter accompanied Miss Gear to New York City. The teacher enrolled Peter in a boarding school. Belle found employment with Mrs.

Gatfield of Nassau Street.

Mrs. Gatfield and her friends held prayer meetings on the city street corners, hoping to convert people to religion. Because Belle was eager to serve God, she gladly joined the group. Her beautiful voice drew many people to hear her sing and speak.

Two years later, Belle joined another religious group. She went to work for its leader, Elijah Pierson. After several years, this group moved to a country estate called the Kingdom. Belle, the only black member, went too. Although she had given the group all her savings, she soon discovered she was not being treated as a member. Instead, she was expected to do all the household chores.

There were many quarrels among leaders of the Kingdom, and ridiculous claims of being sent by God to set up His Kingdom on earth. One member, Matthias, insisted that he was Jesus Christ, re-born. When Mr. Pierson died suddenly, the group broke up. Belle was relieved to part company with these "false prophets" and return to work in the city.

She soon found work with the Whiting family on Canal Street. A short time later, newspapers reported that Mr. Pierson of the Kingdom had died from poisoning. Matthias, the most fanatical member of the Kingdom, was accused of murder. He was tried and acquitted. Then Mr. Folger, another member, accused Belle of the supposed murder.

Now the newspapers said that "a colored woman"

was suspected. No arrest was made. Nevertheless, Belle was greatly upset. She felt she must prove her innocence. She contacted former employers, including Isaac Van Wagener and John Dumont. All wrote letters praising Belle's virtue, honesty and industry.

Then a surprising thing happened. Mr. Gilbert Vale, a newspaperman, believed that Belle was being unfairly accused because she was black. He made a thorough investigation of the case. Belle was completely cleared.

Encouraged by Mr. Vale's report, Belle sued Mr. Folger for slander—attempting to ruin her good name. Again she won a legal case against a white man. The all-white jury awarded her $125.

In the meantime, Peter, now in his early teens, had started roaming the streets with a gang of young Blacks. He began skipping school and lying about it to Belle, Miss Gear and his teachers. Finally, Belle had to admit the bitter truth. The cruel treatment Peter had received in Alabama had changed him from an honest little boy to a youth who believed that lying and stealing were the best ways to get along in a white man's world. Belle tried to reason with him, but this didn't change Peter. His new friends had more influence with him than she did.

Peter was finally expelled from school. He came to Belle whenever he was in trouble with the police. In desperation, she went to Peter Williams, a Negro barber, who tried to help black youths stay out of trouble. Mr. Williams gave Belle little hope. The city, he told her, was filled with white men who couldn't find jobs. An uneducated black youth, especially one with a police record, had no chance of finding work. He advised signing Peter up to serve on a whaling ship. Negroes usually made up over half the crew.

The next time Peter was picked up by police, Mr. Williams agreed to pay his fine on one condition—Peter must ship out within a week.

Peter sailed from New York City aboard the whaler *Zone of Nantucket* in 1839. About a year later, Belle received a letter from him. He spoke of the difficult, dangerous life aboard the ship. And he asked about Diana, Elizabeth and Sophie. Then he begged Belle's forgiveness for all the trouble he had caused her.

Belle felt hopeful. Perhaps away from the bad influences of the city, Peter might still become a good man. Mr. Whiting answered Peter's letter for her. Then he wrote another letter to Belle's daughters. They would be happy to have news of their brother.

During the next year, two more letters arrived from Peter. Then they stopped coming. In vain Belle inquired about the whaler *Zone*. At last she gave up hope. She feared that the ship and its crew had been lost at sea.

❖❖

Belle had been in New York City ten years now. She had known only hard work, worry and grief during those years. Here, in the city, Peter had got into trouble. Here, too, Blacks and Whites walked the streets, hungry and homeless. And here, illegal slave traffic was carried on, its

Belle says good-by to Peter.

miserable victims chained in filthy cages near the docks until they could be smuggled South and sold. Many people who claimed to be religious knew of these evils. Yet they seemed to care not one bit.

Mr. Whiting seldom talked about religion. Yet he felt sorry for the city's poor. Frequently he gave Belle a half-dollar when he left for work in the morning. "Here, Belle," he said, "if some poor fellow comes asking for a job, have him clean the walks and give him this." After he left, Belle cleaned the walks herself and pocketed the coin. Later she added it to the growing hoard in her mattress. Once again, she was saving to buy a house. Now that Peter would not be returning, she wanted to have her daughters with her as soon as possible.

One morning, a ragged old man asked for work. Belle turned him away. She watched as he hobbled down the street, weary and discouraged. He reminded her of her father. Suddenly she felt guilty about the coin in her pocket. The Quakers in Ulster County had lived by the Golden Rule: "Do unto others as you would that they would do unto you." But she, Belle, was becoming as bad as the city people who shut their eyes to suffering. "The rich rob the poor, and the poor rob each other," she said to herself.

She went to her room and prayed for forgiveness and guidance. Soon it was clear to her what the Lord wanted her to do.

CHAPTER EIGHT

Sojourner for God

Early the next morning, Belle came downstairs with her few belongings in a pillowcase.

"What's all this, Belle?" her employer asked.

"The Lord has given me a new name, and I'm to walk the land telling the people about God and doing His work."

"What's your new name?"

"Sojourner." Belle spoke the word with pride. She had often heard it read from the Bible. A sojourner stayed a short time in one place and then moved on. This was what Belle intended to do. She would travel about "exhorting the people to embrace Jesus and refrain from sin."

"Do you have any money?" Mr. Whiting asked.

"I have twenty-five cents," Sojourner replied. "There's a heap more upstairs in my mattress. I'd be obliged if you would give it to the poor."

Sojourner stepped out of the house and headed

down Canal Street, leaving the old name and the old life forever. The day was June 1st, the year 1843. She must have been about forty-six years old.

Without looking back, she hurried toward the East River. The coin in her pocket paid for a ferry ride to Brooklyn. From there, she took the rising sun as her "guide and compass."

A great thankfulness filled her as she left the city and swung out into the open country. She lifted her voice in her favorite song.

At noon, she stopped at a farmhouse and asked for a drink of water. A Quaker woman came out and drew water from a well. As she lifted the dripping bucket, she asked, "What is thy name?"

"My name is Sojourner."

"That's an odd one. What is the rest of it?"

Sojourner was confused. As a slave she had used her master's name. "I don't know," she admitted at last.

The gladness had gone out of the day. "Oh, Lord," she prayed as she trudged along, "I need a handle for my name."

"Truth!" The word flashed into her mind. *"I am the Way, the Truth, and the Life."* God's name was Truth, and God was now her master. "Sojourner Truth," she said joyfully. She would bear the God-given name proudly as she walked the land showing God's truth to the people.

Toward evening, a man stepped out of a farmhouse. "Are you looking for a place to work?" he called.

Sojourner hesitated. "I am doing the Lord's work," she called back.

"Then stop here. My wife is ill and we need help."

Sojourner hadn't eaten since morning. She was tired and hungry. Thankfully she accepted the man's offer. She stayed a few days, caring for the sick woman and her family. When the woman was better, Sojourner prepared to leave. "Stay with us," the husband urged. "We will pay you well."

"I must be about the Lord's work," Sojourner said, picking up her pillowcase. She refused the handful of coins that the man held out to her. Instead, she took twenty-five cents. "This is enough," she said.

She traveled on across Long Island, caring for the sick or doing housework in exchange for food and a place to sleep. She never accepted more than twenty-five cents for her services. To her, the hoarding of money now seemed evil. She was doing the Lord's work, and the Lord would provide for her needs.

Sometimes she stopped at homes, asking for a place to sleep. Because she was black and a stranger, she was often turned away. If darkness overtook her and there were no houses near, she slept under the stars. At times, her twenty-five cents paid for a night's stay in a tavern. But usually someone was eager to give her food and shelter. If she was offered a loaf of bread and a wedge of cheese to eat along the way, she accepted gratefully. The rich, she discovered, seldom had anything to give; but the poor were happy to share the little they had.

This tall, gaunt Negro woman, clad in her long black Quaker dress and white shawl, wearing men's cast-off shoes or no shoes at all, was a rare sight. Curiosity alone drew people to her. It was unusual for a Negro to speak before a group. Then, too, during this period of the nation's history, entertainment of any sort was scarce.

They came, expecting the comic performance of an end man in a black minstrel show. But they soon learned that Sojourner was no comedian. This woman with the God-given name possessed a dignity and a confidence unusual in anyone, especially in a Negro who had suffered under slavery.

Although she probably spoke in ungrammatical English flavored with Negro dialect, the magic of her deep, rich voice held her listeners spellbound. She sang hymns she had learned in church, and others she had made up herself. And she spoke of the evils of slavery, and of the sin existing in the great city she had so recently left. She pleaded for mercy for the poor and down-trodden. And always her message was the same: "If you want to serve God, you must do good to His people."

At last she left Long Island, and crossed by boat into Connecticut. There were many religious camp meetings held in the East at this time. She frequently attended these huge, outdoor gatherings. They usually lasted several days. Families camped in fields, living in wagons, tents or huts. They spent their time listening to speeches, singing, and sitting around on boxes, sharing their views on religion.

Sojourner was becoming well-known. Now the words, "Sojourner Truth is coming!" ran ahead of her. She found crowds at the camp meetings waiting to greet her. Although she was a Negro, they listened with great respect and interest as she spoke and sang.

Sojourner enjoyed these meetings. Her dark eyes twinkled as she spiced her talk with a clever story. But her broad, sensitive face grew sad as she told of the suffering among the poor. She often sang of the glory land where the weary and oppressed could lay down their burdens and rest.

After she spoke, she sat around with the others, exchanging ideas about God and Jesus. People seemed especially interested when she told of the day the Lord had appeared as a great light and stopped her from returning to slavery.

As she walked from meeting to meeting, one thing troubled Sojourner. She had left New York City without getting in touch with her girls. They must be worried about her. When someone offered to write to them, Sojourner accepted thankfully. In the letter she told her daughters of her love for them. Then she explained about her new name, and how she was now doing the Lord's work.

Hoping the girls would understand, she continued on her way. As her audiences grew, Sojourner's faith in herself, and in her power to interest her listeners, grew also.

One evening at a meeting in Northampton, Massachusetts, Sojourner's faith in God was put to the supreme test. About one hundred white youths rushed into the camp grounds as the meeting was about to begin. They raced around, overturning wagons and ripping down tents. The terrified people scattered, hiding wherever they could find cover.

Sojourner, the only black person there, was probably the most terrified of all. She had seen white mobs attack Negroes. And she had no doubt that this gang would take fiendish delight in torturing—even killing—her. Her fright carried her to the far side of the grounds. Here she hid in a tent behind a large trunk, hoping for a chance to escape to a nearby field.

The mob drew near. "Burn the buildings!" a rough voice shouted. "Fire the tents!"

Sojourner shook with terror. She was about to make a dash for safety. Then she thought, *Why should I run and hide? Me, a servant of God?*

She stepped from the tent. Walking tall and unhurried, she climbed to the top of a small hill. About her stretched the wide fields; above her shone the full moon.

The rioters rushed toward her, waving sticks and clubs. Sojourner watched them come. Then slowly she lifted her face to the bright sky. Raising her arms, she began to sing the song she loved. Her clear sweet voice soared above the uproar:

As the rioters rushed at Sojourner, she raised her arms and began to sing.

It was early in the morning
Just at the break of day,
When He rose, when He rose, when He rose,
And went to heaven on a cloud.

She finished and looked down into the faces of the youths crowded around her. "Why do you come at me with sticks and clubs? I am not harming you."

"We ain't going to harm you, old woman," someone shouted. "We want to hear you sing. Tell us your experiences."

She talked and sang of the goodness of God. And she told of the long-ago auction, and of the Neelys, and of the scars on her back. She told about Ma-Ma Bett, Baumfree and her small son, Peter. The mob listened without interrupting. Some wiped away tears. At last she grew tired. "If I sing one more song, will you leave us in peace?" she asked.

"Yes! Yes!" they shouted. "Sing one more song." She sang. Then, true to their promise, they left quietly. The meeting continued without further trouble.

CHAPTER NINE

The Lord's Most Important Work

Sojourner had covered many miles and attended a number of camp meetings. The people at these camps treated her with great respect. And they gladly shared their food and living quarters with her. But she was beginning to wonder if they were really doing the Lord's work. They seemed mostly interested in saving their own souls and in getting to heaven. They seldom talked about helping their fellow men. And the suffering of slaves caused them little concern.

Finally, Sojourner decided that she must find a place where she could rest and wait for further instructions from the Lord.

Friends directed her to the Northampton Association located at Florence, Massachusetts near Northampton. This was a community, or commune, of educated people who were trying to make the world a better place.

They hated injustice in any form. Because they were concerned about abolishing, or doing away with, slavery, they called themselves abolitionists. There were not many abolitionists in the United States at this time. Many people hated them and considered them troublemakers.

Sojourner found them living together in an old factory at the edge of town. Here they raised silkworms and wove silk cloth for a living. They lived very simply. Everybody worked. Sojourner joined the group and served as laundress for the community. Soon she became a loved and highly respected member. She made many friendships that were to last the rest of her life.

Among these friends were such famous abolitionist writers and speakers as Parker Pillsbury, William Lloyd Garrison and Frederick Douglass, an escaped Maryland slave.

The Association had no single religion. Some members were Quakers. Some belonged to a religious group called Seventh-day Adventists. Others had broken with their churches because their ministers upheld the rights of wealthy slaveholders.

Garrison was especially bitter. He lashed out against people who called themselves Christians yet kept humans in chains. "Prejudice against color is a sin against God!" he declared in his weekly antislavery newspaper *The Liberator*. Because of his outspoken views, Garrison had been dragged through the streets with a noose around his neck by a mob of wealthy "Christian" gentlemen who threatened to hang him.

But this rebellion against churches didn't bother Sojourner. Hadn't she herself frequently lashed out at churchgoers. "How can you expect to do good to God unless you learn to do good to each other?" She even developed a deep and lasting affection for Parker Pillsbury who claimed not to believe in God. Years later she said, "If Parker Pillsbury was an infidel, then I wish the world was full of such infidels. Religion without humanity is poor stuff."

Although Sojourner couldn't read, she possessed a remarkable memory. For some time, she had been attempting to memorize the Bible. At Northampton she was able to continue this project. She preferred to have little children read to her. They patiently repeated verses as often as she wished, and they didn't attempt to explain the meaning as adults insisted on doing. Then she could say the words over to herself when she was alone, and arrive at her own meanings.

In 1846, Sojourner's quiet, pleasant life with the Northampton Association ended. There was not enough silk business for the community to pay its debts. The group broke up. Although members continued their fight against slavery, the factory was no longer their headquarters.

Sojourner remained in Northampton for several years, working as a live-in servant once again. She was waiting for instructions from the Lord. In the spring of

1849, Sojourner made a trip to Ulster County to visit Diana, her oldest daughter, who was ill. Diana, now 34, was still living at Dumonts' and planned to remain there. Sophie and Elizabeth, both in their early twenties, had married and moved out of Ulster County. Dumont had given his permission.

When Sojourner returned to Northampton, she found that Samuel Hill, a friend from the Association, was building a small house for her. She was too old to walk the

The children read the Bible to Sojourner so she could memorize it.

roads, now, he told her. She needed to settle down and live in one place.

Sojourner wasn't sure that she wanted to settle down. Friends were calling her "Auntie Sojourner" or "Old Sojourner," and she had a few white hairs. But she didn't feel old. And when instructions came from the Lord, she must be free to leave. Then, too, she had wanted a home mostly because of her family. Now her girls had places of their own.

She had just settled into her house when Olive Gilbert, a friend, called on her. Briefly Miss Gilbert described an autobiography Frederick Douglass had written, telling of his experiences as a Maryland slave. This account, or "narrative," Olive Gilbert said, was moving hundreds of Northerners to support abolition.

Would Sojourner be interested in publishing her story as a northern slave? "You must realize, of course," Miss Gilbert warned, "that such a book can be a two-edged sword." She explained that when Douglass confessed in his book to being a fugitive slave, he became a hunted man. He had to escape to England until friends could raise money to buy his freedom from his Maryland master.

Sojourner was legally free, but hers would be a story of northern slavery. Northerners might be embarrassed and angered at being reminded that the despised practice of owning slaves had existed until recently among them.

The idea delighted Sojourner. If her story would help free the millions of slaves in the South, she would gladly risk having it appear in print.

The *Narrative of Sojourner Truth: A Northern Slave* appeared in 1850. Sojourner was about 53 years old at the time. William Lloyd Garrison arranged for the printing, and also advertised the book in *The Liberator*.

Booksellers had welcomed Douglass's book, but

they refused to stock this story of a northern ex-slave. They were sure it wouldn't sell. It seemed that if Sojourner's book was to reach the public, she must peddle it herself.

Too old to walk the road? Sojourner shrugged her shoulders. With a light heart, she filled a carpetbag with copies of the *Narrative*, plopped her old sunbonnet on her graying hair and stepped out of her house. She locked the door and returned the key to Samuel Hill. Long ago she had promised to do the Lord's work. Now she was convinced that the Lord's most important work was to free the slaves in the South. Perhaps her book would help.

CHAPTER TEN

Women's Rights

Mr. Garrison advised Sojourner to travel to antislavery meetings and sell her book during intermissions. He and other abolitionists would keep her supplied with copies, he told her. At first, she traveled in Massachusetts. She had many abolitionist friends there. They were always willing to open their homes to her. And, if the distance was great, they drove her by horse and buggy to her next meeting place.

At the Northampton Association, Sojourner had heard talk of women's rights. Now many of her abolitionist friends were discussing this new movement. Women, they said, as well as slaves, were treated unfairly. No state allowed women to vote. In many states, a woman could not even own property. If she worked outside the home, her wages were paid to her husband.

But as Sojourner moved from place to place, her thoughts were mostly about slavery, which was now a burning issue in all the states. Fearing slaves would be freed, the South was threatening to separate from the North and set up its own government. To prevent this,

Congress in 1850 passed the Fugitive Slave Law.

This law placed heavy fines or imprisonment on anyone caught helping a slave to escape. Even a freed Negro in the North could be dragged back into slavery if one white man and one white witness swore that he was escaped property. The slave by law could not defend himself. Frederick Douglass, now legally free, said bitterly that he could be returned to slavery "on the oath of any two white villains." Many northern Blacks moved into Canada to prevent being seized and made slaves again.

Few laws were more frequently broken. Many Northerners who had never taken a stand on slavery now became strong abolitionists. The Underground Railroad moved several hundred slaves to safety in Canada. This system was neither "underground" nor was it a "railroad." It gained this name because escaping slaves were called passengers; the homes or barns where they were sheltered, stations; and those who guided them, conductors. Many Quakers were active in this movement.

The only slave Sojourner ever freed was her son, Peter. But her *Narrative* was selling well and turning many Northerners against slavery. Most people in the North didn't resent the book as Miss Gilbert had feared. Instead, they welcomed it as a powerful antislavery weapon.

In October 1850, friends encouraged Sojourner to attend a women's rights meeting in Worcester, Massachusetts. There she joined a group of antislavery speakers led by the English abolitionist, George Thompson. She traveled with them into New York State. At first she appeared only during intermissions, selling her book. Then, one day, Mr. Garrison opened the meeting. After a few remarks, he said, "And now my friend, Sojourner Truth, will address you in her own peculiar fashion. Wendell Phillips will follow."

Sojourner was panic-stricken. She had never appeared before such a large crowd. And to be followed by Wendell Phillips, the brilliant, renowned speaker! Why he would put her poor performance to shame!

Slowly she mounted the platform. She sang one of her songs. Then, briefly but sincerely, she told of her experiences as a slave. When Wendell Phillips got up, he said, "I can add little to what Sojourner Truth has already told you. So I will merely repeat in my own words what she has said so well."

It was Sojourner's simple, heart-felt message, not Mr. Phillips's polished speech, that charmed the audience. People crowded around her to congratulate her and buy her book.

From that day, Sojourner often shared the platform with famous speakers. They said, "We reach the minds of our audiences, but Sojourner touches their hearts. When she speaks, her listeners ask themselves, 'What if slavery had happened—not to some poor black person—but to me?' "

When anyone commented on Sojourner's amazing ability to influence her listeners, Sojourner said, "God speaks through me."

About this time, people began requesting copies of Sojourner's pictures—shadows she called them—and copies of her songs. She was already having notices, or broadsides, printed, announcing her lectures. Now she had pictures and songs printed, too. They cost her very little, and she sold them for a few pennies each. The profits from these and from her book covered her expenses. Now, occasionally, she traveled by railroad.

Perhaps this was how she managed to get as far as Akron, Ohio in May, 1851, to attend the Woman's Rights Convention in the Old Stone Church. Abolitionists and workers for women's rights had people in Ohio in a state of anger and confusion. Women at the convention were working mainly for the right to vote. Many people, especially men, were greatly opposed to rights for women.

Sojourner wasn't welcome. The women were horrified when the tall, ex-slave, wearing Quaker clothes, a sunbonnet, and lugging her carpetbag, marched down the aisle. When she sat down on the pulpit steps, they turned to their leader. "Don't let her speak, Mrs. Gage. It will ruin us. Every newspaper in the country will mix our cause with abolition and niggers. We'll be denounced."

Mrs. Gage, the women's rights leader, was also a

strong abolitionist. She was well aware of Sojourner's power to influence her listeners. Now she said calmly, "We'll see when the time comes."

The meeting went smoothly until the second day. Then a group of ministers planted themselves in the audience for the purpose of making fun of these "unwomanly females."

The clergy shouted down each resolution presented, especially the one on the right to vote. They insisted that women were inferior to men both mentally and physically; therefore women needed to have men take care of them. Christ, they pointed out, was a man. They added that Eve, the first woman, was responsible for bringing sin into the world. Because of her—a woman—man had been thrown out of paradise. Men in the audience shouted and cheered.

The women had lost control of the meeting. Not one had the courage to stand up to these ministers. But Sojourner remembered how preachers often twisted the meaning of the Bible to favor wealthy slaveholders. Now these clergymen were using the same trick to put down women.

Sojourner glanced at Mrs. Gage. The leader nodded. Sojourner laid her sunbonnet aside. Hisses and jeers accompanied her to the platform. But with her first words, a hush fell on the crowd. Her powerful voice carried across the auditorium to people gathered outside.

"Well, children," she began, "where there's so much racket there's bound to be something out of kilter. I think between the Negroes in the South and the women in the North, the white man will be in a fix pretty soon."

"That man over there," she continued, "says that women need to be helped over ditches and into carriages and given the best places. And aren't I a woman?" She bared her right arm to the shoulder. "Look at me. Look at my arm! I have plowed and planted and gathered into barns, and no man could head me. And aren't I a woman? I could work and bear the lash as well. . . ."

"That little man in black there," she said, pointing to another minister, "he says women can't have no rights, cause Christ wasn't a woman. Where did your Christ come from? From God and a woman. Man had nothing to do with it."

Then with keen wit she drew upon her superior knowledge of the Bible to prove false each statement made by the ministers. Deafening applause followed nearly every remark.

At the end, she defended Eve. "If the first woman ever made was strong enough to turn the world upside down all alone," she said, "these here together ought to be able to turn it back again. And now that they're asking to do it, the men better let 'em"

She raised her hand to hush the applause. "Obliged to you for hearing me, and now Old Sojourner hasn't got nothing more to say."

The old black woman had turned the tide in the women's favor, and they were deeply grateful. Many who had feared to have her speak became dear friends of hers for the rest of her life. And they became strong supporters of abolition as well.

"And aren't I a woman?"

CHAPTER ELEVEN

The Sword Is Drawn

For two years Sojourner traveled throughout Ohio, pleading for women's rights and a peaceful end to slavery. Gratefully she accepted the loan of a horse and buggy to carry her over rough country roads. When she reached a crossroad, she slackened the reins and said, "Lord, you drive." She insisted that God always guided her to a place where she had a good meeting.

Sojourner had talked to God as she walked the roads. Now she talked with Him as she jolted along in the high-wheeled buggy. She felt sure that slavery could be ended without violence.

But the patience of many abolitionists was wearing thin. Since the Fugitive Slave Law, an embittered Frederick Douglass was seeing a great deal of a white abolitionist, John Brown. John Brown cried out that violence was the only possible way to end slavery.

One day, Sojourner attended a meeting where

Douglass was speaking. She sat in the front row, listening intently. Douglass's voice broke as he described thousands of his race attempting to reach Canada, only to be dragged back, beaten, tortured, chained and sometimes branded. Nothing, he said bitterly, could end slavery but violence and bloodshed.

Slowly Sojourner rose to her full height. She pointed a finger at her fellow ex-slave. Her vibrant voice thundered through the auditorium. "Frederick," she demanded, "is God dead?"

Instantly the gloom lifted. Despair gave way to hope. If enough people spoke out, the government would have to listen. Victory might still be won without bloodshed.

The antislavery struggle moved westward to the Kansas-Nebraska territory, land that had not yet been made into states. The Missouri Compromise stated that slavery should be barred from both Kansas and Nebraska. But Congress, influenced by powerful slaveholders, agreed to let settlers vote on the issue.

"There's no question about Nebraska," Garrison said. "Slavery hasn't a chance that far north. But Kansas is right next to the slave state, Missouri. There's going to be trouble in Kansas!"

As the antislavery struggle moved west, so did Sojourner. In 1856, she attended a Friends of Human Progress Meeting in Battle Creek, Michigan. She liked this midwest community so much that she made a small down payment on a house at the edge of town. Then she sent letters to her daughters, urging them to join her.

Soon Elizabeth, now widowed, and her young son, Sammy Banks, left the East to make their home with Sojourner. They brought Sojourner's oldest grandchild, James Caldwell, with them. Sophie and Diana remained in the East.

Battle Creek was a strong abolitionist center. When Sojourner wasn't traveling, she frequently visited the Merritts, a Quaker family in downtown Battle Creek. Their home now served as headquarters for many powerful abolitionists.

It was at the Merritts' home that Sojourner first heard of Abe Lincoln, the young, politicking lawyer from Illinois who spoke out boldly against slavery. She felt a deep kinship with Lincoln. They had both known poverty, hard work and sorrow. He, too, believed in speaking the truth in simple words, and people were beginning to listen to him.

Lincoln stated his views on the Kansas-Nebraska Bill. "Anyone with a grain of horse sense can see what's going to happen. Free men and slaveholders can't live side by side. They'll be at each others throats before you know it."

Lincoln was right. Abolitionists rushed in hoping to keep Kansas free. At the same time, slaveholders swept in from Missouri, terrorizing settlers in an attempt to swing votes in favor of slavery. In 1856, a local war broke out.

One town was burned to the ground.

To Sojourner, the Bible spoke of brotherly love. But John Brown, Douglass's friend, received a vastly different message. He and his sons moved into Kansas to "do the Lord's work." Shouting, "God cries out for blood!" they murdered five proslavery men. Even Frederick Douglass called it "a terrible remedy for a terrible malady."

Abolitionists worked harder, hoping to keep Kansas free. Now about sixty years old, Sojourner carried her "testifying" against slavery into Ohio, Indiana and Illinois. Friends worried about her. These states had many "nigger-haters" eager to tar-and-feather some unwary victim.

"Children, don't worry none," Sojourner said. "I expect the Lord will take care of me." She refused to carry a weapon, but she now carried a heavy cane. "Could be mighty fine for cracking heads," she commented.

At last, it seemed that Kansas would be saved for free men. Weary of traveling, Sojourner returned to Battle Creek. She looked forward to settling down and enjoying her family and friends. She lived in the center of town now. The Merritts had given land and had a small frame house built for her and her family. It was located on College Street, near the Merritts' home.

Mr. Dumont had moved west. After he left Ulster County, Diana, too, joined her mother. But Sammy Banks was Sojourner's greatest joy. She loved this little grandson as dearly as she had once loved her small brother, and her son, Peter.

James Caldwell, now a teenager, seemed a little ashamed of this odd grandmother who attracted so much attention with frank opinions. But Sammy listened carefully when she told of the cruelties of slavery. He, at least, understood why Sojourner had to speak out against this unjust system.

Sammy was in school and learning to read. Eagerly he searched the newspapers for stories about Abraham Lincoln to share with his grandmother.

Sojourner followed Lincoln's political career with great interest. Although he wasn't an abolitionist, he regarded slavery as a great evil. He was gaining many supporters because of his antislavery stand. Sojourner was delighted when she learned that he might be nominated for President.

Then, in a move that outraged abolitionists, the United States Supreme Court declared that slavery couldn't be barred from any territory. A short time later, John Brown struck at Harpers Ferry, in western Virginia. He and a small band of followers succeeded in capturing weapons and ammunition from the federal arsenal there, but they failed in an attempt to arm the many Negroes in the area. Brown was captured and condemned to die.

His final words touched the hearts of all people

Sammy listens to his grandmother tell of the cruelties of slavery.

who loved freedom and justice: "I pity the poor in bondage that have none to help them. It is my sympathy for the oppressed and wronged who are as good as you and as precious in the sight of God . . . Had I interfered in behalf of the rich, the powerful, the intelligent, or the so-called great, every man in this court would have deemed it an act worthy of reward rather than punishment."

The following year Abraham Lincoln was elected President. Soon after his election, the slaveholding southern states pulled away from the North, or the Union. They set up their own government called the Confederacy. By April, 1861 the Civil War had begun. For years Sojourner had hoped that slavery could be ended without war. But maybe this, like making the Neelys good, was too big a job—even for God.

Lincoln declared that the purpose of the war was to keep the southern states from pulling away, or seceding, from the United States. It was also being fought to keep slavery from spreading into new territories. He said nothing about freeing the slaves.

Abolitionists were outraged. Lincoln should free all slaves at once, they said. Sojourner preached patience. She had great faith in Lincoln. He would free the slaves when the time was right. Now she said to her abolitionist friends in Battle Creek, "Just wait, children. It takes a great deal of time to turn this great ship of state around."

In September, 1862, Lincoln issued an Emancipation Proclamation. Slaves were to be freed on January 1, 1863.

By the President of the United States of America.

A Proclamation.

Whereas, on the twenty-second day of September, in the year of our Lord one thousand eight hundred and sixty-two, a proclamation was issued by the President of the United States, containing, among other things, the following, to wit:

"That on the first day of January, in the "year of our Lord one thousand eight hundred "and sixty-three, all persons held as slaves within "any State or designated part of a State, the people whereof shall then be in rebellion against the United States, shall be then, thenceforward and "forever free; and the Executive Government of the "United States, including the military and naval "authority thereof, will recognize and maintain "the freedom of such persons, and will do no acts "or acts to repress such persons, or any of them, "in any efforts they may make for their actual "freedom.

"That the Executive will, on the first day

One day, Josephine Griffing, an abolitionist friend, stopped in Battle Creek. "Sojourner," she said, "the war isn't going well. We desperately need you." Although Sojourner hadn't wanted the war, she was beginning to feel that maybe this was her battle, too.

Within a few hours, the two women were heading for Angola, Indiana, where proslavery people had taken the law into their own hands. Self-appointed law officers stopped the two women at the border. They were allowing no Negroes to come into the state, they said. However, by federal law, Sojourner had a right to enter. Using the buggy whip and Sojourner's cane, the two women fought their way across.

They made several attempts to hold meetings in the open. Angry, lawless mobs broke them up. At last, Sojourner arranged a meeting in Angola's town hall. "Nigger-haters" threatened to burn the building. "Then I'll speak on the ashes," Sojourner declared.

As the crowd gathered, there were shouts of "Lynch the old woman!" and "Blow out her brains!" Ignoring the guns and knives in the audience, Sojourner took her place on the platform. Soon the heckling stopped, and the meeting continued without trouble.

Ashamed of their cowardice, local abolitionists and law-abiding citizens of Angola came out of hiding and took a stand for justice. Local police attempted to throw Sojourner in jail for disturbing the peace. Because she had broken no law, federal officers rushed into Angola and came to her aid.

**Law officers tried to stop Sojourner Truth and her
abolitionist friend, Josephine Griffing.**

The two women continued their speaking tour of
Indiana. For a time, the old black woman bravely faced
the threats and the danger. At last, she could endure it no
longer. She became seriously ill. Mrs. Griffing took her
home to Battle Creek to be cared for by her family.

CHAPTER TWELVE

The Great Man and the Tragic Hour

For many weeks, Sojourner was close to death. But when spring came, she was up and about "budding out with the trees," she said. Soon she was working as she had so often before, doing laundry and housework for white families. Sometimes, she and Sammy picked wild berries and peddled them around town.

Her thoughts were often with Abraham Lincoln who had done so much for her people. And she wondered about the newly-freed slaves. Uneducated and penniless, how were they getting along?

Early one June morning in 1864, Sojourner arrived at the Nortons' home where she was to do the laundry. "I've got to hurry with the washing," she said. "I'm leaving for Washington this afternoon."

"For Washington!" Mrs. Norton exclaimed. "For heaven's sake, why are you going to Washington?"

"I'm going there to advise the President!" Sojourner said proudly.

Sammy went with her. They traveled by train, in carriages and on foot. They had many friends to visit and meetings to hold along the way. Sojourner was a celebrity now. Her name was known throughout the United States and Europe. An article praising her had recently appeared in *The Atlantic Monthly*, an important magazine. Harriet Beecher Stowe, a famous abolitionist author, had written the article.

They reached Washington in the fall. Crowds were celebrating two recent important victories over the southern armies.

Sojourner and Sammy stood for a long time in front of the Capitol building. Sojourner's thoughts traveled back to Ma-Ma Bett weeping for her "lost children," and to Baumfree, abandoned to die by those he had served so faithfully. She felt again the cut of Neely's rods and recalled the scars on her little son's body. At last, God had sent a Moses to lead her people from bondage. He had given them Abraham Lincoln.

"Sammy," she said as tears streamed down her cheeks, "you see that flag on top of the Capitol? Well it don't mean *scars* and stripes for black folks anymore. Now it means stars and stripes for all us children of God."

They stayed with Lucy Colman, an abolitionist friend who was arranging for Sojourner to see the President. In the meantime, she and Sammy walked the streets to see how the ex-slaves were getting along. They were horrified by the filth and squalor. Thousands of bewildered Blacks, mostly from Virginia, had rushed into

"Massa" Lincoln's city, expecting the glorious freedom they had dreamed about. Hundreds more arrived daily.

But the city had no way of caring for these masses. Sojourner found them crowded in makeshift barracks, shacks and tents. Many lacked light and heat. Roofs leaked, and the smell rising from rotting water-soaked floorboards and muddy, littered yards was almost unbearable.

Late in October, Sojourner gained admittance to the President. He greeted her with great kindness. "I have heard of you many times," he said. He took a large, beautiful Bible from a shelf. "This was given me by the colored folks of Baltimore," he told Sojourner.

She opened the velvet cover and stroked the pages with careful fingers. Here were the words she loved so much—and could not read. She thought of the law that had made it a crime to teach a slave even the ABC's.

When it was time to leave, she reached in her carpetbag for her autograph book which she called her *Book of Life*. She also kept letters and newspaper clippings in it. She watched with pride while the hand that had signed the death warrant of slavery, wrote: To Aunty Sojourner Truth, Oct. 29, 1864, A. Lincoln.

Sojourner thanked him and said, "Mr. Lincoln, I'm sorely troubled. I think of you as Daniel thrown into the lion's den. I'm afraid the lions will tear you to pieces."

Abraham Lincoln smiled. "Well, they haven't done

Sojourner meets President Lincoln.

it yet, Sojourner," he said. But the smile couldn't hide the sadness on his careworn face.

Sojourner left his presence, knowing she had made a friend.

Lincoln had set up a Freedmen's Bureau to help solve the Negroes' problems. In December, Sojourner was hired by the Bureau and paid a small wage to work with the women at Freedman's Village. This was located at Arlington, Virginia, across the Potomac River from Washington, D.C. Newly arrived ex-slaves were housed in barracks there. Sojourner was to provide "intellectual, moral and religious instruction."

Filth had always been a part of slavery. Now Sojourner went from family to family. "Be clean!" she ordered. "Cleanliness is next to Godliness!" She taught mothers to wash clothes, scrub floors, comb hair and sew on patches. She had already enrolled Sammy in Freedman's Village school. Now she insisted that mothers enroll their children, too.

One day, Sojourner learned that landholders from Maryland were stealing children to be used as slaves. If mothers protested, they were thrown into jail. She appealed to Captain Carson, head of the village. Nothing could be done, he said.

Sojourner was very angry. She had great faith in federal law. It had helped her; it would help these mothers. "You are free! You have rights! The law will stand by you!" The next time slave snatchers raided the village, the mothers fought them off.

Sojourner threatened to report the kidnappers to federal authorities. The men turned on her. "Old woman," they said, "we'll have you thrown in the guard house for meddling in our business!"

"You dare to try that," Sojourner thundered, "and I'll make these United States rock like a cradle!"

The men never returned. They were convinced that the angry black woman would carry out her threat.

On April 9, 1865, General Lee, leader of the southern armies, surrendered at Appomattox Courthouse. The war that was to have ended in a few weeks had lasted four years. Over half a million lay dead.

April was a time to bury hatred. But six days later, black flags fluttered in the spring breeze. Abraham Lincoln had been killed by an assassin's bullet.

Long lines of mourners filed through the East Room of the White House, past the coffin of the dead President. Sojourner passed with the rest. Her dark eyes held the ancient sorrow of her race as she paused for one last look at this great man who had been her friend.

Of all her sorrows, this seemed the hardest to bear. Who would care for her people now? Who would have their interest at heart? Sojourner had learned long ago that the best cure for sorrow is work. Now she decided that she could best honor Lincoln by renewing her efforts to help the freed slaves.

She returned to Freedman's Village to find the ex-slaves hiding in their barracks. They feared that they would be returned to slavery, now that Lincoln was dead.

"You are free," Sojourner assured them. "You can't be made slaves again."

In September of that year, Sojourner was assigned by the War Department to work as a nurse at Freedman's Hospital in Washington. She was nearly seventy now. Nevertheless, she often walked great distances in the city, doing errands for the wounded soldiers.

One day, she decided to ride on a streetcar. In the past, each route had one car for blacks, the Jim Crow car. With the law ending discrimination, the Jim Crow car had been removed. Blacks and Whites were to ride in the same cars. Angered by the law, conductors seldom stopped for Blacks.

On this particular day, three cars passed Sojourner. As a fourth one approached, she screamed, "I want to ride! I want to ride!" Her screams stopped traffic, and she managed to climb aboard. The conductor threatened her, but she refused to get off.

Not long after that, she was returning from Georgetown with Laura Haviland, a white worker at the hospital. Mrs. Haviland signaled a car. When it stopped, Sojourner jumped on quickly. The conductor pushed her aside. "Get out of the way and let the lady on," he ordered.

"I am a lady, too!" Sojourner replied and headed

Although the conductor threatened Sojourner, she refused to leave.

for a seat. The conductor slammed her against the door. A sharp pain pierced her sholder. "Please take the number of this car," she said to Mrs. Haviland.

At the hospital, Sojourner learned that a bone was dislocated. She appealed to the head of the streetcar company. With his encouragement, she sued for assault and battery. The conductor was fired.

Several days later, Sojourner saw two black women waiting to ride. The driver stopped the horses. "Step aboard, ladies," the conductor said grumpily.

Sojourner was delighted.

CHAPTER THIRTEEN

Peace Brings Problems

But for every problem solved, there seemed to be a hundred more with no solutions. This new-found freedom for Sojourner's people was closer to a nightmare than the fulfillment of a glorious dream.

When Sojourner and Laura Haviland were free of hospital duties, they helped Josephine Griffing of the Freedmen's Bureau hand out clothing to the thousands of unwanted, homeless and hungry ex-slaves. Many were dying from disease and starvation within the shadow of the Capitol building.

Black children prowled dark alleys, stealing to keep alive. Eight and nine-year-olds were arrested and jailed. However, even jail was better than life on the streets.

Sojourner pitied the grown-ups, but these young criminals troubled her deeply. They were the products of America's greed and America's mistakes. And they and their children would help shape America's future. Somehow they must be saved.

Lincoln had believed that the one hope of Blacks lay in education. Sojourner went to General Howard, head of the Freedmen's Bureau. She suggested that the government build schools where Negro youths could be housed and taught blacksmithing, carpentry and other trades.

Together they presented the plan to Congress. Congress wasn't interested. They talked to influential citizens who could persuade Congress. Few of these people were interested, either. The Blacks had caused the country enough trouble. They had their freedom now. Let them look after themselves.

Sojourner was furious. Couldn't these educated Whites understand that schools cost less than prisons and poorhouses?

While Lincoln was President, Congress had talked of giving land, tools and mules to ex-slave families. But the new President, Andrew Johnson, returned all abandoned and captured lands to former owners. Nothing remained for the Blacks.

Nevertheless, many ex-slaves returned to the South. Their lives there had been better than life in the city's slums which were filled with disease and crime. Some returning Blacks were greeted by bullets. Others were put to work as sharecroppers. The Blacks did the farm work, and were supposed to receive a share of the crops they raised. Usually, the white owners took most of the crops. There was little or nothing left for the black families.

The Whites in the South made their own laws, keeping Negroes in slave-like conditions. If a Black managed to own a house, it was burned to the ground. If he sent his children to school, they were terrorized by grown white men. If he tried to vote, he risked being tarred and feathered.

One thing was clear to Sojourner: this freedom— North or South—was leading nowhere. "Oh, Lord," she prayed, "how can I help my people?"

While she waited for an answer, she walked the streets, looking at the beautiful federal buildings. They had been built by her own ignorant, half-starved people. Slaves had lifted the heavy marble slabs, yet they had never been paid for this, or any other, labor.

Again she went to General Howard. "Our blood and tears have been sacrificed on the altar of this nation's greed. Some of its dividends must surely be ours."

Then she told him of another plan. Congress was giving millions of acres of western lands to wealthy men for the purpose of developing mines and building railroads. Why not repay the ex-slaves by giving them land in the West and providing them with farm tools and teachers? "That way they can become self-respecting, self-supporting citizens," she said. "Keeping black folks on charity with nothing to do degrades them worse and worse."

General Howard gave her little encouragement. Only Congress could give away government land, he told her. And the present Congress showed little interest in helping Blacks.

But Congress was elected to serve the people, Sojourner reasoned. What she needed were people to back her plan.

Theodore Tilton, editor of the newspaper, *Independent* drew up a petition and had many copies made. She would need thousands of signatures, he told her.

In February, 1870, Sojourner and Sammy set out to collect signatures. Sammy was eighteen, and Sojourner was in her seventies. Friends claimed she was in her nineties. She didn't deny it; she had no proof of her age.

They started in Rhode Island. A large crowd gathered at the first meeting. Sojourner described the terrible conditions in Washington and then said, "Won't you sign my petition? We've earned land for homes and it would be a benefit to all of you." She got hundreds of signatures. After a few more meetings, she and Sammy hurried back to Washington.

Andrew Johnson was no longer President. Sojourner met with Ulysses S. Grant, the new President. He hastily signed her *Book of Life* and turned to other business. She had no opportunity to tell him of her plan or show him the signatures on her petitions.

Congress, however, greeted her graciously. Fifteen senators signed her *Book of Life*. But only one, Charles

Sumner of Massachusetts, was willing to support her campaign to provide lands for ex-slaves. "If you hope to influence Congress," he told her, "you'll have to get thousands and thousands of signatures."

For three years Sojourner and Sammy traveled, collecting signatures. She pleaded with friends to carry petitions, too. But now that slavery was ended, even former abolitionists were losing interest in the problems of Negroes. At times, Sojourner grew very tired. Without Sammy's encouragement, she might have given up.

By the spring of 1874, Sojourner's carpetbag was bulging with signed petitions. She and Sammy returned to Washington. Sojourner tried to get in touch with Senator Sumner who had promised to present her petitions to Congress. He had died a few days before they arrived. Sojourner was shocked and confused. Before she could plan her next move, Sammy became seriously ill with a high fever. She took him back to Battle Creek immediately. But he failed to improve. He died in February, 1875.

Throughout Sammy's illness, Sojourner had suffered from huge sores, or ulcers, on her legs. These, and the grief over Sammy's death, were more than she could endure. She, too, became very ill. Her daughters called in Dr. John Kellogg, a famous Seventh-day Adventist physician who had recently moved to Battle Creek. Under his care, Sojourner gradually improved.

When her strength returned, she began lecturing

again. Now in her eighties, Sojourner spoke in thirty-six Michigan towns in one year. She talked for women's rights, prison reform and rights for black people. Closest to her heart was the cause she and Sammy worked for together. But Sojourner knew it was useless to take her petitions to Washington. The city was filled with ex-southern generals and southern politicians. They, and Congress, had no interest in justice for Negroes. At least Sammy had never known that their dream had ended in failure. Sojourner was grateful for that.

Sojourner enjoyed watching the neighborhood children at play.

One day, Sojourner received news that gladdened her heart. Thousands of freedmen were leaving the South and moving to Kansas. They were doing for themselves what Congress had refused to do. Now, Sojourner had one last trip to make. She must go to Kansas to see how these people were getting along.

She found that Kansas was giving them land for homes and farms. The law protected their rights. They were allowed to own property, vote and send their children to school.

Satisfied, she returned home, and spent many hours with friends and with Elizabeth and Diana. James Caldwell was living and working in town. This one remaining grandson was no longer ashamed of his grandmother. He visited her frequently.

Sojourner often sat on her doorstep, watching neighborhood children play. Some of them were black. These children would never know the auction blocks or the cut of a master's whip. Their mothers would never look at the stars and grieve for babies sold away. Some of the Lord's work had been done, and she had helped to do it. God was not dead. Much more needed to be done for black people, but as long as God lived, there would be others to carry out His work.

Sojourner Truth died at her home on November 26, 1883. She was probably about eighty-six. Elizabeth and

Diana were with her when she died. Nearly a thousand people, both Blacks and Whites, were gathered for the funeral. A long procession followed the hearse to Battle Creek's Oak Hill Cemetery where she was buried close to her beloved grandson, Sammy Banks.

Each year many people visit her grave. The spot is marked with a slender, six-foot, white marble shaft bearing this inscription:

In Memoriam
SOJOURNER TRUTH
Born a slave in Ulster County,
New York, in the 18th century.
Died in Battle Creek, Nov. 26,
1883. Aged about 105 years.

"IS GOD DEAD?"

Index

118

119

children sold, 16; gets freedom, 20–21; becomes ill, 29; dies, 31
manufacturing, 19
Maryland, 74, 78, 102
Massachusetts, 73, 80, 111
master, 11, 12, 14, 15, 16, 18, 27, 30, 38, 43, 46, 50, 51, 66, 114
Matthias, 60
Merritts family, 90, 91
Michel, 16
Michigan, 89, 112
Missouri, 89, 90
Missouri Compromise, the, 89
Mohawk Indians, 16
Moses, 99

Nancy, 16
Narrative of Sojourner Truth: A Northern Slave, 78–79, 81
Nebraska, 89
Neely, John, 22, 24, 26, 29, 30, 33, 50, 72, 99
Neely, Mrs., 24, 25
New Jersey, 19
New Paltz, New York, 32, 53, 54

New York City, 55, 59, 61, 62, 69
New York State, 14, 19, 20, 35, 82
Northampton Association, 73, 75, 76, 80
Northampton, Massachusetts, 70, 73, 75, 76
Norton, Mrs., 98

Oak Hill Cemetery, 115
Ohio, 83, 88, 91
Old Caesar, 16, 20, 40
Old Stone Church, 83

Peter (brother), 11, 12, 14, 16, 18, 21, 29
Peter (son), 42, 44, 53, 54, 55, 56, 57, 58, 59, 61, 62, 64, 72, 81, 92; sold to Dr. Gedney, 44–45; recovered by Belle, 55–57; works on Roundout Creek, 59; goes to school in New York, 59; gets in trouble, 61; sails on whaling ship, 62
Phillips, Wndell, 82
Pierson, Elijah, 60
Pillsbury, Parker, 74, 75

ABOUT THE AUTHOR

ALETHA JANE LINDSTROM says about herself: "I live in Battle Creek, Michigan, the town Sojourner Truth called home during the last twenty years of her life. I've written short stories and poetry, and have had numerous articles published in periodicals, including *Parents* and *Reader's Digest.*

"I taught elementary school for several years in La Grange, Illinois before moving to Battle Creek where I served as library coordinator for elementary schools in Lakeview, a suburb of Battle Creek. Most recently I was a student teacher-coordinator for Western Michigan University at Kalamazoo where my husband is a professor in the education department. We have one son, Tim, a lawyer in Charlottesville, Virginia.

"This is my first book for children. I decided to write it one evening when I visited Sojourner Truth's grave in Battle Creek's Oak Hill Cemetery shortly after finishing her narrative. As I stood there in the moonlight, reading the inscription on her tombstone, Sojourner seemed very real to me. I felt that children everywhere should have a chance to read the fascinating, inspiring life story of this remarkable black woman."

ABOUT THE ARTIST

PAUL FRAME was born in Maryland, went to school in eight different states, and finally wound up in New York where he stayed. He attended Columbia University and the National Academy of Art. He was a fashion artist and an advertising illustrator before he turned to book illustration, and he has taught art. And for relaxation, it's more art: painting, sculpture, woodcutting—he enjoys experimenting in all media.